10 Keys to Happiness

10 Keys to Happiness

Ancient Wisdom Made Easy

B. BROWN

SCRIVENER BOOKS, INC.

Ten Keys to Happiness
Copyright © 2011 by B. Brown.

All rights reserved. No part of this book may be reproduced or transmitted in any form or by any means, electronic or mechanical, including photocopying, recording, or by any information storage and retrieval system, without written permission from the author.

First edition published 2011.

ISBN: 978-0-9829017-0-0

Cover credits: (leather textures) iStock©Linleo, and RDStock. Photomanipulation by Michael Rohani.

The Fell Types (body text and ornaments) are digitally reproduced by Igino Marini. www.iginomarini.com.

Book design by DesignForBooks.com

Printed in the United States of America.

Contents

Introduction — vii

ONE: Embrace Your Limited Time — 1

TWO: Choose Real Freedom — 7

THREE: Pursue Your Calling — 15

FOUR: Cherish Family and Friends — 23

FIVE: Live in the Present — 31

SIX: Be Virtuous — 39

SEVEN: Love Yourself — 49

EIGHT: Love Others — 57

NINE: Believe — 65

TEN: Take Action — 73

Epilogue — 79

Introduction

Happiness is the meaning and the purpose of life, the whole aim and end of human existence.
— ARISTOTLE

Why did you pick up this little book? You probably opened it up for the same reason I wrote it: to be happier.

We all want to be happy. It is our ultimate goal and purpose in life. It is our nature to want to live well and flourish. No sane person consciously wishes to be unhappy.

And yet, even though we all strive for greater well-being, there is tremendous unhappiness. Just look around, it doesn't take a Gallup poll to see that people are distressed. Tens of millions of us take anti-depressants and anxiety medication. Tens of millions eat their way into morbid obesity. And tens of millions of people can't sleep through the night.

The rest of us may not be taking pills or waking up in the middle of the night, but we are not as happy as we could be. Our busy lives make us distracted and stressed. Every day events, deadlines and responsibilities consume our time, leaving us hoping for that pause that never comes, that moment when we can gain control of our lives, figure it out and be happy. We keep hoping.

In the meantime, we spend our time focused on frivolous things. Some of us take it further, obsessing about our appearance and what others think of us. We are imprisoned by anxiety. We have doubts about whether we are faking it, whether we will be found out. To numb ourselves we turn to food, drugs and alcohol — anything to distract us from a few moments with ourselves when we might have to confront our weaknesses.

And look at our goals. It seems our society is more obsessed than ever with fame, fortune and power — all of which have nothing to do with happiness. Our heroes are sports and Hollywood stars who often end up in tear streaked television confessions or mug shots.

The media provides nonstop coverage of the famous, the rich, the sexy and the outrageous. But don't blame the media, they are a market driven animal that only produces what gets our attention and what sells products. The media just reflect the fact that we are obsessed with momentary pleasures and distractions.

We aim at the wrong goals and result is obvious: unhappiness and even despair. These feelings may not always be obvious or apparent, but they are there. They are there in the quiet moments when we wonder what we are doing with our lives, what our purpose is, and why we aren't happier. We distract ourselves with everyday tasks and deadlines and suddenly our time is gone.

As Augustine said, "Man wishes to be happy even when he so lives as to make happiness impossible."

So what can you do? The answer is surprisingly straight-forward. First acknowledge that your goal, your ultimate goal in life, is to be happy. Next, determine what you need to do to become happy. And, finally, do it.

Sound easy? It isn't. But that's why this little book is here, to help. We'll review what ten things you can do to become happier.

What Happiness Is Not

But before we do that, let's pause for a moment and review what we mean — at a high level — by happiness.

What is happiness?

Let's first look at what happiness is not. Don't confuse happiness with pleasure, a brief moment of good feeling — happiness is more than just a feeling. And be on the look out because pleasure comes in many forms. We're not just talking about physical pleasure like eating candy or having sex, but any kind you might feel: the comfort of money, the thrill of fame, the exhilaration of power, and the self-satisfaction of people admiring or envying you.

Happiness is not the pleasure you feel when you buy a new car or piece of clothing. It is not the first few weeks of a new relationship when you think you found your soulmate. It is not reaching the top of your career — with everyone looking on wishing they could be you.

Happiness is not becoming a CEO. It is not a Swiss bank account. It is not a box of chocolates.

It is not becoming a CEO. It is not winning the World Series. It is not a Swiss bank account. It is not a gold record. It is not tenure at Harvard. It is not being elected to Congress. It is not sex with a super model. It is not a box of Godiva chocolates. It is not winning an Oscar. Ultimately, these things, while impressive, are not a condition of happiness.

That may seem odd, but think about it. When you are facing death, are any of those things going to be important to you? No. That means something else should be the focus of your life. The goal should not be reaching the heights of society or status. It should not be power, money and fame.

Well then, what about love? Many people confuse happiness for the early stages of love — another form of pleasure. They think that if they could only find their true love, they would be happy the rest of their lives. There's no denying that early on in a relationship the rest of the world and all its problems melt away. We are focused on the other person and forget or suppress any feelings of unhappiness. But any one experienced in relationships knows that this phase of love always passes, followed by dishes, laundry, finances and all the normal stuff of life.

Ultimately all these things we are discussing are momentary pleasures, and while they may make you feel good, they are not fundamentally going to develop a profound sense of well-being, or happiness.

To help explain, imagine if you could hook your brain up to a machine that releases dopamine — the chemical that creates a sense of well-being and power. This chemical is produced when people take cocaine or exercise heavily. Let's say you could pump this into your brain 24/7. Would you be happy? You would certainly feel good, but you wouldn't be happy, just distracted by pleasure. Eventually you would feel empty, longing for something more. As we shall see, our human nature, the preprogramming in our brain, demands much more of us.

Despite this, it is important to note that happiness and pleasure are not always disconnected. It is pleasurable to become a CEO or win the World Series and these things can also contribute to your happiness if you have the right perspective. If these achievements were sought just to obtain money, fame, power, or further inflate your ego, they will not contribute to your happiness. But if running a company or being the best ball player in the world are the side-effect of your striving for excellence and living life well, they will — as we shall see — be one contributing factor to your happiness.

Likewise, relationships and love, which are kinds of pleasure, also contribute to your happiness. After the early euphoric phase of a new love, true love takes root with genuine acceptance of the other person. This kind of love is just one element of what can make us happy — and we'll talk more about that later.

What Happiness Is

Understanding the meaning of happiness is no easy task. Even the origin of the word helps cause confusion. The old English definition derives from "hap," meaning chance or good luck. So you see, we have strong associations with the word relating to whether something happens to us by chance. But in true happiness, as we shall see, luck only plays a small role. We'll learn that real happiness depends less on chance and more on our actions, what we choose to do.

The ancient Greeks had a better word for happiness, eudaimonia, which meant living successfully, doing well in life, flourishing, and thriving. But don't worry too much about these definitions right now; we'll be reviewing it throughout this little book. A true understanding of what it means to be happy develops with time, with experience, and with action.

A good starting point for us is Aristotle, an early Greek philosopher. He explains it best. He said wishing to be happy is like wanting to be good at something. Let's say you wanted to be a concert violinist. If you spend all your time thinking how great it will be standing in front of the crowd and soaking in the applause, you'll never get there. You need to practice, practice, practice. The applause is a side-effect of the work, a side-effect of being excellent at something — and ultimately you'll recognize it's the excellence that improves your well-being, not the applause. Similarly, if you spend all your time wishing you were happy, but doing nothing about it, you will get nowhere. You must labor at it, and happiness comes as a side-effect. You must take action. Form new habits. And live differently.

The following ten keys are meant to help guide you in this process. The wisdom is well tested. It is largely pulled from early Greek philosophy (mostly Aristotle), Eastern philosophy, Christianity, Judaism, and Buddhism. After you've learned and acted upon these ten keys, you'll have a better understanding of the complexity of happiness. Intellectually understanding these rules is only part of it. You must live them. And in living them you will be building a happy life.

After some time you will come to see that that true happiness is about an enduring sense of well-being or living well. It is about living your life in a certain way, by acting in specific ways — as defined in these ten keys. It is about not just surviving and getting by or achieving certain pleasures. It is about, as Aristotle explains, flourishing by employing your unique abilities to their fullest. It is about being comfortable with yourself. Loving yourself. Forgiving yourself. Respecting and accepting yourself. Loving others. Forgiving others. Being in the moment. Acting virtuously. Achieving authentic freedom. Pursuing your true calling and excellence. Working so that you can look back at the end of your life and quietly acknowledge that you lived well. The cliché is true: Happiness is the journey, not a destination.

The alternative is to have your life pass by, consumed with petty and insignificant desires and wants — to waste your life.

So chose the other path and get started.

ONE

Embrace Your Limited Time.

Do you love life? Then do not squander time; for that's the stuff life is made of.
— BENJAMIN FRANKLIN

I believe that the very purpose of our life is to seek happiness.
— THE DALAI LAMA

You will die.

That may seem an odd way to begin a discussion about happiness. But acknowledging your limited time is the essential starting point on your path to well-being.

Why? Becoming happier requires active and willful work. If you don't acknowledge that your life may end at any moment, the work of becoming happy can be put off for another day, and another and another, until it's too late.

We Are Lazy

We are all lazy to some degree and we prefer pleasure over discomfort. So when confronted with a task that requires effort and discipline we prefer the easier path (namely, the couch). That's true even if we know the more difficult path will bring more benefit to us in the future.

It is difficult to be motivated to act, unless you are aware that inaction will bring grave consequences.

Dieting is a good example of our natural laziness. Most of us have tried or know people who have tried to diet. It starts with an internal commitment to yourself that "today is the day I begin my diet." And within a short period of time you're confronted by the bonbon. The brain immediately rationalizes, "Well, it is small and I only just started this silly diet, so it's not like it's damaging my progress. So why not?" Down goes the bonbon. Then over the coming days and weeks several other thousand calories slide down your throat, rationalized in a similar manner.

The diet is ruined by a thousand small steps because you couldn't keep focused on your long term goal. The end result: Your weight goes up or stays the same. You are defeated again. You're confidence is reduced, making each new attempt all the more difficult.

But consider this. Imagine you're in a doctor's office, sitting on the bench in your paper gown. The physician returns and looks down. "It doesn't look good," he says. You start to think he's talking about cancer or some other disease your behavior may not be responsible for. He says, "If you don't lose 20 pounds, you will die in a matter of months — the weight is straining your weak heart."

There it is. You've got it: a timeline. Time is no longer ambiguous. You no longer have forever. When you've got "forever" to do something, why impose discipline and take action today? It's much easier to think about getting disciplined at a later date and swallow that bonbon. But with the doctor's information, if you don't take action right now, you will face consequences that are slightly more unpleasant than being denied that bonbon. Each time you pick up that bonbon you can now pause, look at it and ask: "What is more important two seconds of slight pleasure on my taste buds or an early death." The choice is easy. The discipline comes. The weight falls off.

The diet struggle is no different from any path to betterment, including greater happiness. If the consequences of not acting are grave, then the choice to act is easier.

How Much Time Do You Have?

So now imagine this. You've reached old age, near the end of your life. This perspective, looking back at your life, is the only one that allows you to see your life in its entirety. This is the kind of thinking Aristotle and other Greek thinkers encouraged. In looking back, imagine that an honest answer was that your life was not a happy one — or not as happy as it could have been. That would be a tragedy. Your one life, the one that was given to you and shall never be repeated, could have been happier.

But here's the twist. You don't know when you'll die. Humans are fairly optimistic creatures, so if you're like most people you're probably figuring that you'll check out somewhere around the average, 77 years of age. But the fact is, you could die anytime. Next week. Tomorrow. After you finish reading this sentence. Surely the people who die in car crashes aren't thinking in the morning while they are brushing their teeth that today is the day — they wouldn't be worrying about preventing tooth decay.

Our perspective on death is twisted. Americans are specialists at glossing over death and imagining it only happens to old folks or that it is an event in the unimaginably distant future. We are experts at not thinking or talking about death. It is kind of a national taboo. After all, we are supposed to have the good life here, enjoying our things and reveling in our success. The American ethos dwells on the possible and focuses on being optimistic about the future — while these are good things, sometimes we take it a bit too far. Thinking about death seems out of character.

So let's remember our poor friend in that doomed car. Death comes at anytime. Those are the facts.

Now, if that is true, doesn't that change your perspective on happiness? If you learned that you had one week to live, you'd think differently. You'd think about how best to live those last few days? You'd think about everything you've been doing wrong? You'd think about how trivial your daily concerns are? You'd realize that many of your goals are misdirected? You'd think about the things you wished you'd done but never did. You'd reach out to those around you to tell them that you really did love them?

And that's just the point. If you don't know how much time you have left, five days or five decades, you had better start thinking about how you want to live your life. And one of the easiest conclusions you can draw, is that you want your remaining time to be happy.

But just like our friend the dieter, it is difficult to get motivated to act — to work toward a happier life — unless you are aware that inaction will bring grave consequences. The fact is that if you do nothing, you may well be on your way to having lived an unhappy life. And that is true whether you live five days or five decades.

Act Now

Because you don't know how long you have to live, you must act today. Vigorously pursue happiness. How? Follow these keys.

You can start by acknowledging and *embracing* your limited time. Realize death comes at anytime. Don't obsess about it; get active about it. Be happy that you are one of the few that are aware of this fact and willing to change — instead of marching forward in life like a robot.

This is often how those who experienced near-death experiences decide to live their life. They look at each day as a gift.

Continually check yourself. As Aristotle suggests, imagine yourself at the end of your life looking back. Would you be pleased with the decisions you made today?

Happiness is about action. It is about making the right choices in the time you have left. The following nine keys are here as a guide to help you.

In Review

1. Acknowledge that life is temporary.
2. As Aristotle suggests, view your decisions as though you were standing at the end of your life looking back.
3. Remind yourself to live in the present.
4. Don't obsess about your limited time; embrace it.
5. Don't just think about it; act upon it.

TWO

Choose Real Freedom.

It is the nature of desire not to be satisfied, and most men live only for the gratification of it.
— Aristotle

Liberty is the right to choose. Freedom is the result of the right choice.
— Anonymous

Freedom. To be happy you need to be free. That's obvious. The Declaration of Independence even declares our right to pursue life, *liberty* and *happiness*.

It is a simple concept. Your happiness is in danger if you don't have basic freedoms: an ability to move about at will, marry who you want, choose your own profession, say what you think or even have as many children as you desire. In countries all over the world these freedoms are restricted.

We Live Imprisoned

So, as the cliché goes, we Americans are lucky. We can do anything we want, anytime we want. We've got freedom. So why spend another word discussing it?

We do have freedom, that's a fact. But the vast majority of us are living our lives in a kind of prison of our own making. We are not as free as we think. And, consequently, we are not as happy as we should be.

What does that mean? How can we not be free? And why aren't we as happy as we should be?

The process starts very early in our childhood. We are bombarded by images and messages about what we need in order to be happy. The television, friends and family tell us that in order to be happy people need things. And so you pick up the line: "I would really be happy if only I _____." You fill in the blank.

> *Buddha learned that we are not free, but that we are all imprisoned by our endless cravings or desires.*

As a child you begin to wish for things. You want a special toy car, a bike, a book, a popular friend, some candy, a horse, and on and on. As you move into adolescence you fixate on getting that special girlfriend or boyfriend, getting into the right school, buying a car, being popular, being attractive and on and on. In our adult lives, it continues. You want the perfect mate, the best job, gobs of money, a life of leisure, to be the envy of your neighbors, to get exciting sex (with or without your spouse), to be in total control of every situation and on and on.

If you summed it all up, you could say that your life is consumed by desires. Desires for things, money, sex, power, appearances, brains, status, control and/or fame. We're all different so we all want different things, but we all have one thing in common: desire. We are a consuming animal. We are constantly on the prowl trying to satisfy our desires. That's because we are never satisfied.

We always want more. Just observe those around you. Read the interviews with the supermodel who wishes she didn't have certain flaws, that her hips were smaller or her lips more full. See the newspaper story about the entrepreneur that sold his company for $10 million. Suddenly he wants to start a new company so he can hit $100 million. And after he attains that he wants to break the $1 billion mark. Look at the Hollywood stars that make a blockbuster movie and become overnight sensations. They spend the rest of their lives trying to repeat the feat and remain the center of attention of our national media machine. Some of them go on and on, devising new stunts to keep in the limelight, as their bodies decay and they pull their flesh tighter and tighter to remain appealing.

Now look at us normal folks. We may not have such grand ambitions, but we are still consumed by unending desires. We think: if only I could buy an SUV, if only I could lose 20 pounds, if only I could get that promotion, if only my nose were smaller, if only I was the one always invited to those parties, if only I could make six figures, if only I had a bigger apartment, if only I wasn't so anxious, and so on. Most of it is vanity, silly vanity.

Our advertising industry picks up on our dissatisfaction. Just look at the ads around you. Beautiful, sexy people entice you from magazine pages and billboards. Men walk around bleary eyed wishing they could have sex with these goddesses and women stumble about miserable that they will never be that desirable. Every imaginable new product pops up on television or in the store aisles. The message is clear. Your life will be easier, better — dare we say it, happier — if only you could own this new and improved blender.

We spend our short lives fixated on these silly desires. We are working longer hours than our parents to try to attain things. Both spouses tend to have careers now. We spend all year waiting for that week off or earning enough to get that new car.

We spend our entire life in pursuit of the *things* that will supposedly make us happy — instead of spending our entire lives in pursuit of happiness. We are imprisoned by our own desires. We have so many choices, so much freedom, and so many wants, we are running like madmen trying to satisfy ourselves. We are that large hamster running in his wheel. And there's the catch: we won't ever be satisfied. It is like a great cosmic joke that's been played on us. Suddenly, our time is up. Life is over.

Does that sound like freedom or happiness? No.

Trapped by Desire

This view is not new. Both Buddhists and Christians recognize the problems that absolute freedom can create. Buddha, for example, spent years wandering about trying to find the answers, trying to discover how to become content and happy. He found what he called his "Noble Truths." Essentially, what he learned was that we are not free, but that we are all imprisoned by our endless cravings or desires. These unsatisfied desires make us unhappy.

Buddha's answer was to eliminate these selfish cravings by creating new habits and desires. He taught that people should spend their lives changing the way they see, think, speak, act and live. He showed people how to become more mindful — or how to live in the moment (see Key Five) — through patience and meditation. Ultimately, Buddha wanted to free you from your ego, to control desire, ambition and pride. These keys are focused on a similar task.

Plato, an early Greek philosopher, described how most of his colleagues were trapped, following desires and wants that would never make them happy or free. They were living in a world of shadows, not realizing what was real and false. His answer was to use reason, like we are here, to understand this and escape from it.

The Christian approach is similar in many ways to the ancient Greeks and Buddhists. They sum up their belief in a simple phrase: "The Truth shall set you free." Their assumption is similar: You only think you are free right now, but you are in fact imprisoned by your desires, by your absolute freedom that your endless cravings produce.

To help explain, think of a small child. Imagine he is given total freedom by his parents. He can come and go as he pleases. He has access to any kind of food or candy. He can go to bed when he wants and play video games until he drools. That child is not free. He is a slave to his desires — like some rat running from sugar bowl to sugar bowl. If his parents love him, they would say no and impose limits. Then his slavery to desires is lifted and he is truly free.

The Christian answer is similar to this, replacing your unbounded and false freedom with a limited or real freedom. You turn away from the unlimited freedom of chasing any and all worldly desires and you exchange it for an authentic freedom, a limited liberty, of restricting and controlling your desires — instead of having them control you.

Christians teach that faith in God, "the Truth," shall truly free you from superficial desires. You replace it with true love, acceptance and forgiveness. You give yourself up, ego, petty desires and all. You exchange it for what seem to be the restrictions of belief and faith. But instead, what you find is real freedom, freedom from your former prison cell of desires.

Another very important point about this more authentic, limited freedom ("the Truth"), is that *you are not in control*. You never were and never can be. Good or bad things happen to you and you can only do your best. Understand that and accept it and it is freeing. In fact, that is true freedom.

Whether you choose the Greek, Christian, Buddhist or another path, the key point is to recognize your current state of imprisonment. You need to recognize that most of us have a superficial understanding of happiness, one that is essentially defined by our ability to achieve pleasure and avoid pain. We define pleasure as sex, money, appearances, leisure, fame, etc. We define pain as the opposite or the absence of these things.

You need to acknowledge that many, if not all, the goals that are programmed in your head are setting you up for an endless and fruitless pursuit, ending in a life of unhappiness.

If you are unhappy in your old house, you will be an unhappy person in a new home. If you finally do get to have sex with 100 supermodels, you will be a tired unhappy person. If you do get that nose job, you will be a beautiful unhappy person. In fact, a recent study from Harvard University showed that people are never as happy as they'd imagine they'd be once they got the thing they wished for. Think of an example: Everyone in the family really wanted that new car. It was all they could think about. Three weeks after it arrives, it's covered in food and nobody cares anymore.

Another good example is weight loss. Many people imagine: "If only I could lose 20 pounds, I'd look better and feel happier." Before they were fat they thought eating would bring happiness. After they were fat they think losing weight and looking better will bring happiness. They never take a moment to realize that the pleasure of food or the feeling of being attractive are superficial desires that imprison them. They don't focus on the real issues: Most overweight people assume they are unhappy *because they are fat*. The fact is that most of them are fat *because they are unhappy*. In other words, before they got fat, they were unhappy. If they confronted their real problem, their unhappiness, weight lose becomes a possibility.

Get Control

You must review your life and examine what is motivating you to live the way you do. You need to develop new habits and goals. It sounds easy, but it's not. Use these keys to focus on what is important in your life. Is it superficial things, like appearances, material goods or sex? No. Your freedom comes from acknowledging that what is important is loving yourself, loving others, living in the moment, pursuing your true calling, acting virtuously, cherishing family and friends, and so on.

As Aristotle suggests, you must be able to answer the following question correctly: In my life, did I pursue things of importance or fleeting desires? Am I a human being with dignity, or am I an animal?

You need to acknowledge how you've spent a lifetime learning to chase the carrot. It takes months and years of training yourself out of your reflexive habits of chasing these cravings.

Let's clarify two points before we leave this section:

Don't misunderstand; some desires can be a very good thing. It is our nature to want to improve our condition, to provide better food, clothing, education and housing for our family or others. The key is to not let your desires control you.

And don't blame capitalism and the consumerist society for spawning all our desires. Like it or not, capitalism is neutral. Remember that it is our decision whether to take the choices that capitalism provides to an extreme or not. When we see outrageous things on TV or see silly products for sale, they are only there because we are buying or choosing them. It is an indictment of our inability to restrict our appetites. Change your outlook and the market will change.

Now it's your choice. Which will it be: Real freedom, or a prison of your own making?

In Review

1. Realize that your desires are superficial. More power, money, status, fame, things, attractiveness, etc., will not make you happier.
2. Acknowledge that you are imprisoned by your desires.
3. Understand that this causes you unhappiness.
4. Take action: Suppress these superficial wants and replace them with goals that will bring you happiness, specifically, the rest of these keys.

THREE

Pursue Your Calling.

He who enjoys doing and enjoys what he has done is happy.
— Johann Wolfgang von Goethe

True happiness comes from the joy of deeds well done, the zest of creating things new.
— Antoine de Saint-Exupery

Each of us is unique. And each one of us has a particular thing that we were meant to do.

One early Greek philosopher, Aristotle, explained it this way: Everything has a function. Take a knife for example. The function of a sharp knife is to cut and cut well.

Just as a knife has a function, so to do other objects, like cups and tables. Similarly, eyes, hands and feet have functions. Everything has a function.

So what then is the function of a human being? What is your function? What should you be doing? What is your calling and why is it connected to your happiness?

It should be self-apparent that doing what fits you is directly connected to your happiness. When you are doing something that uses your abilities to their fullest and it's going well, you are closing in on happiness. If you are doing something that does not interest you, something against your nature or, even worse, something you hate, it is more difficult to cultivate a sense of well-being.

Of course, you may need to take a job just to earn money. Even if that's the case, just acknowledging you are doing it from necessity and pursuing your true calling in your spare time, can contribute to your happiness. Likewise, if you're a bit old to change things, you can always find some spare time to pursue interests that give you more meaning.

 ## Follow Your Nature

So how do you discover what you should be doing? Aristotle partially answers this question by saying that you should do what you are best at. Take a carpenter for example, he should hammer and cut wood if that is what he can become excellent at. Aristotle is also careful to point out that you cannot be happy if you are not performing in a manner that is in line with your true nature. In other words, you may be good at a number of things but you'll only be happy if you are pursuing your true calling.

The question then is whether working with wood is the carpenter's true calling or function. The question also translates to you. What are you currently pursuing in your life. Are you pursuing your true calling?

This is not an easy question to answer. One way of helping you examine whether you are fulfilling your true function is to review some common reasons why most of us are pulled away from what our nature dictates we should be doing.

What Holds Us Back?

As an example, let's say that you had an early interest in photography, law, medicine, acting, painting, motherhood, furniture making, or you name it. But over the years you were never really able to pursue it. Life slips by and you never bother to act on your intuition. Why?

One of the most common reasons we let our dreams go is our belief that we must first be *responsible*. We tend to be exceedingly pragmatic and practical. How can you pursue your true calling if others duties call? How can you choose the life of an artist, when everyone expects you to go to law school? Or, alternatively, how can you possibly spend all that time and money on law school when you should be advancing in your current career for the sake of your family? Many people view their true callings as frivolous and irresponsible. Often, they do not see how they could possibly make enough money doing it. The irony here is that doing what you love, means you do it well, which means you will probably be rewarded beyond just your love of the subject.

> *The only people who do not fail are those that do nothing.*

Another major motivating factor keeping us from fulfilling our natures is *fear*. We all face fear at times in our lives. Sometimes we aren't even aware of it, as it works its way into our subconscious, quietly telling us we can't possibly do what we are contemplating. Other times it is there in the open, yelling at us, telling us to stop and go back to what is familiar. God forbid we should try to reach our dream only to find out we aren't capable. Isn't it much better to keep living our life of quiet desperation? Risk, fear tells us, is our enemy. Risk means failure is a possibility. Unfortunately, all true change is marked first and foremost by risk and the possibility of failure. The only people who do not fail are those who do nothing.

Laziness is fear's partner, working hand-in-hand to inform us that we will never get around to fulfilling our goals. Laziness keeps us on our current trajectory. It is so much easier to do what we know. Change is not only marked by risk but by hard work. Change means having to do things we aren't familiar with or things that we need to work hard at to master. In other words, it requires some suffering. For example, a good body comes from the pain of working out or a good mind comes from the difficulty of studying. So laziness drugs us into resisting that change, sitting on the couch, mechanically executing our routine and avoiding our true calling. And the more distant we get from what we love, the less we feel like doing anything.

You might not expect *vanity* to pop up here as a major obstacle to your true calling. But think about what decisions brought you to chose your current goals in life. For many of us, we are strongly influenced by what those around us think of our choices. Think of parents, friends, colleagues, spouses or significant others. Many of us have spent years working to attain a certain level in chosen paths. You may have a certain level of respect or salary. How much admiration will an established lawyer garner when he tosses it all in to be an artist? How easy is it for a doctor walk away to become the best mother possible? These issues of the ego create obstacles to fulfilling what is truly right for us.

There's even a less obvious cause to straying from your path: *thoughtlessness*. It is kind of comical, but many of us are so caught up in the day-to-day business of lives that we fail to stop and take an accounting of what is going on. We just don't think about whether what we are doing is the best possible thing for ourselves. It is a kind of thoughtlessness. We may have passing thoughts about being tired or unhappy, but we fail to sit down and say, "I am profoundly unhappy doing what I am doing, and I need to make some changes." The longer you go on, the more tired you get and the less likely it is that you will pause and contemplate all this.

And then of course there's *talent*. What if you just don't have the talent to do what you wish you could do? To go back to our knife example: Even though you really wish you could be a knife, you may not be very sharp. First you should be aware that a lack of talent is a good indication that you may be headed in the wrong direction. You may need to think about what other talents you have. These undiscovered talents, when found and deployed, will bring just as much satisfaction. In other words, you may wish you could be the best lawyer possible, but your real calling is counseling.

A second point is that talent is not always necessary. Many people achieve much with little talent. Persistence is often much more important than talent. Persistent actors, for example, often rise much faster and higher than talented ones. Again, back to our knife example, suffice it to say that even a dull knife can cut through things as long as it saws long enough. If that works for you, go to it.

And this is just what the latest genetic studies suggest, that "success" at virtually any task, from violin playing to rock climbing, is more about putting in the practice (some suggest more than 10,000 hours) than about some innate genetic gifts.

All of these issues we've just covered are obstacles on the path to finding your true calling. A theme that can run through all of them is *how you view yourself*. If you have a lowly view of yourself, it can make these obstacles even larger. If you spend a good portion of the day putting yourself down, you are less likely to have the required confidence and courage to undertake risk and change your life.

For most of us, these factors push us unto a different path — a path of less resistance. Isn't it easier to do what others expect of us? It's easier to avoid the comments like, "What makes her think she can do that!?" And that's a comment that can come from a parent or your own head. The result is a withdrawal to the familiar and the safe. It is why Henry David Thoreau, New England thinker and writer, said, "the mass of men lead lives of quiet desperation."

The simple antidote to this is what you're lacking: *courage* — the strength to follow your true calling. And courage comes from a quiet confidence you get when you know, love, accept, and respect yourself — as we'll learn later. You are stronger when you want, but do not need, the love and acceptance of those around you.

 ## Make a Plan

But courage may not be the only issue. Most people are not sure what their true calling is. Some people spend a lifetime searching. The place to start is in your youth. Go back and examine your interests before you and others convinced yourself of another direction.

Ask yourself, at the end of my life I would like to have _____. Finish the sentence. Write out a list of goals. Put them on a time line. What do you want to accomplish in the next month, three months, six months, year, five years, decade, and until the end of your life.

You may or may not find your calling, but you must actively search. You'll make mistakes. The point is to try.

And once you're trying to fulfill your nature, you will become freer and happier. Your conscious or subconscious anxiety and even anger — if you've got some — will subside. Much of those feelings are driven by being a false person, acting in conflict with your nature.

As we explained at the beginning, Aristotle saw happiness as a kind of flourishing that comes from employing your unique abilities to their fullest.

Plato was an ugly, portly Greek man who shuffled around Athens asking people questions because he loved philosophy. People were drawn to him because he was good at what he did.

Doing what you love, and becoming excellent at it, may earn you more money and titles. But that's not why you do it. Money and titles are cold comfort at the end of your life. Do what suits you. That is the key — even if it is in your spare time.

In Review

1. As Aristotle said, every human has a specific function.
2. Is what you are doing in line with your true nature?
3. Have any of the following slowed you down?
    a. Worries about being responsible.
    b. Laziness.
    c. Concern about what people may think: vanity.
    d. A failure to think about your life's direction.
    e. Concern about sufficient talent.
    f. Your view of yourself.
    g. A lack of courage.
4. Take action: Strive to find your calling and create a plan to achieve it.

FOUR

Cherish Family & Friends.

Without friends no one would choose to live, though he had all other goods.

— Aristotle

All who would win joy, must share it; happiness was born a twin.

— Lord Byron

You are not alone. You do not exist on this planet by yourself. What's more, you would not want to exist alone. Even if you could snap your fingers and get everything you desired, you would not be happy by yourself.

After food, water and security, the desire for community is one of man's fundamental needs. It is in our nature to want to be among others. Who you are and how happy you are is largely defined by the relationships you have or don't have.

So what are these relationships? And how do they influence your happiness?

The core relationships around you include your parents, siblings, spouse, children and friends. Chances are that you have some of these, that they aren't all alienated from you or dead.

Relationships We Don't Choose

Let's start with a relationship most of us have had: Our *parents*. This is one of the trickiest of all relationships. We can't fully understand our parents or how they impact our happiness until we become parents ourselves. Then we can truly see how difficult it is to be a parent: to provide, to be fair, to be strict, to love and to ignore rejection. The relationship is complex and contradictory. The extremes of any relationship are represented here: love, anger, joy, rejection, betrayal, loss, accomplishment, etc.

> *A child's endless needs are a crash course in telling you that what matters in life is not you, but the other.*

Parents are different from some relationships because we don't choose our parents. Who raises us is a lottery. Some of us get good parents and some get not so good parents. Some love too much and some love too little. Some are too strict and some aren't strict enough. Some are cruel and some are not, and so on.

No matter how the lottery turned out for you, you cannot allow your relationship with your parents to keep you from becoming happy. That said, there are many ways this relationship can interfere with your happiness.

Consider how you love others. Much of this is determined at an early state in your life. Were you held as a child? Did you know you were loved? Did your parents show their love by devoting themselves to you in some way? It could be that your parents worked very hard to provide for you — even if they weren't there much for you.

The point is that if you entered adulthood sensing or knowing that you were not truly loved or accepted, then it can be a kind of handicap. For example, not being fully loved can reduce your confidence.

And if you are not confident, you are less likely to pursue your true calling (as we discussed in Key Three: Pursue Your Calling). You are less able to resist others who are telling you are not capable of pursuing your dreams. And take, for example, the young girl who is not loved. It is a cliché that she grows up looking for acceptance and love, ending up in teenage pregnancy because she did not respect herself enough to say no.

This is not a free pass to self-pity — quite the opposite. The less perfect your parents were the harder you must work.

The point is this: Nobody has perfect parents. Your parents' parents were flawed. And you will be a flawed parent too. Once you realize that, a burden is lifted. You recognize that you're parents attitude toward you has less to do with you as it does with their own level of self-love, which their own parents helped determine. In this light it is much easier to do what you must do: Forgive. If you truly do forgive, the weight is gone. You are free. And just as importantly, you can look at your parents with compassion for any pain they experienced growing up.

In terms of the importance of relationships, *siblings* are very much like parents. If you have siblings, they probably also did things to injure you — as you injured them. But just like parents, you must acknowledge that in your relatively short life you will intimately know few people. It is also in your nature to care for and love the family. You should go through a similar exercise of reviewing your relationships with your siblings. Give and ask for forgiveness and acceptance, if necessary. There's no need to fall on your knees, just quietly and consistently show that you care.

Relationships We Choose

Now let's look at relationships that are your choice: spouses, children and friends. In a certain sense parents are easier than *spouses*. You only become really conscious of your relationship with your parents around the age of six or so and then twelve years later, you're gone. With a spouse, it's the rest of your life. And if you are not in a loving, caring relationship with your spouse, you will not find happiness.

As many as 50% of marriages end up in divorce. In making the decision to get divorced is the belief that "if only" I found someone who was a better match then everything would be all right. In the vast majority of these cases, a better match has nothing to do with it. Find another mate and they will come with a different set of "problems" you despise. If your relationship is not as good as it should be, it is most likely because you are both failing. (Of course, this excludes physical abusive and other psychotic types.)

The easiest way to illustrate this is to go back to your first date. Think of how you treated each other, with respect, patience, joy, and happiness. That fades in all marriages because we get lazy, because we begin to take the other person for granted, or because we feel we've been wronged and we can't keep giving. And it's guaranteed your partner feels the same way.

If you want a loving relationship, it is pretty straightforward. You've heard it before: You need to work at it. Yes, but what does that mean. Well, love lives in the little things — in the little actions. Did you say, "I love you"? Did you bring her flowers? Did you empty the dishwasher? Did you let him watch the football game? Did you stay home instead of heading out with friends? Did you let him go out with friends? Did you say how much you appreciated her work?

List out five or ten things that make life difficult with your spouse. List out five or ten things you love about your spouse. Have her or him do the same. Sit down and review it. Stop the things that hurt. Review the things you love. Stop hurting the other person. Forgive and accept. Keep the list around and look at it. One of you may be less willing or able to do this because of past baggage. You need to acknowledge that and work harder for the other.

Those feelings you had when you first fell in love will likely never return. Those were not true love anyway. That was euphoria — a joy of newness. Day-to-day familiarity puts a wet blanket on that. One of the obstacles on the way to loving your spouse is to realize that. Realize that true love seeps in after ten or twenty years of marriage. When you can look at your spouse and appreciate that they are with you, regardless of your flaws. Here is a person who has chosen to live and die with you. They care.

Nothing helps that process more than having a child. Having *children* for some is as it should be: a joyful event. For some it is terrifying. Either way, there is no way to anticipate exactly how it changes your life or to understand how limited your life was until you bring new life into this world.

A child is a teacher. The screaming, the feeding, the endless needs are a crash course in telling you that what matters in life is *not you*, but the other. The child teaches you that all your petty, self-centered desires are meaningless. You must care for the other. And over time you come to realize that is were true happiness is. All these years you were thinking you needed certain things to be happy. The child teaches you that giving, selflessly, is the true path to happiness. Loving others is the true path — and children can teach that better than anyone else.

This respect for the other, for life, energizes your well-being. If you begin to treat the child as an accessory, something you were expected to do as part of your life, then you are disrespecting the other. And in so doing, condemning yourself to a life of self-centeredness and unhappiness.

If you are childless, there are plenty of shortcuts to learn to love the other. Of course, you can adopt. But another way is to focus on true friendship.

The Importance of Friends

Friends are another relationship we choose. Very few of us know what true friendship is. We think of friends as someone we get together with to laugh, gossip or have a drink. We think they are people with similar interests. Best friends might be someone we've known a long time.

But true friendship is a rare thing. And it is a requirement for happiness. As Aristotle points out, a dirty little secret is that a lot of our friends serve us in some way. They provide us with some pleasure, connections, or utility, so we work to keep them around. They might get us access to a club or a ballpark. They might have money to loan us. They might have beautiful friends we want to be around. They might do us a lot of favors and so on.

But a true friendship, Aristotle argues, is one in which you have no such requirements. They are not there for you to use. A true friendship is one in which we love the other with no expectation of getting anything in return. In fact, we only wish to benefit the other. We are acting to promote happiness in the friend. Aristotle puts it this way: "The best friend is the man who in wishing me well wishes it for my sake."

What we get out of true friendship is not easy to describe. Suffice it to say that genuine friends are giving you an opportunity to be generous, to be good and virtuous. And in being virtuous, as we'll learn, you become happier (see Key Six: Be Virtuous). So friends, in short, give you the chance to act in a way that serves you both.

So who should be your friend? How should you choose? Naturally, friends should share some interests. But they need to be more than that. They need to challenge and drive you to be better. Your happiness depends on being a better person, on being virtuous. Your true friends should help you rise to new heights.

And remember, you are your friends. You become like those around you. In choosing friends you are choosing what kind of person you are. You can only really be good in the company of good people. And being good means being happy. This is just another way of saying, by choosing your friends, you are choosing whether you will be happy or not. If a person drives you to respect yourself, to love yourself and others, they are your friend. If they are not doing these things, they are using you and you are using them for simple pleasures and distractions from your day-to-day grind. They are merely company to pass the time with.

All of your relationships (parents, siblings, spouses, children and friends) determine who you are and whether you are happy. You have a choice in some of them. Ultimately, you possess the power to determine how these relationships affect you. You have the power to forgive and love. And most importantly, you have the power to give. And that is happiness.

In Review

1. Happiness requires relationships.
2. Parents: Forgive, love and respect them.
3. Siblings: Forgive, love and respect them.
4. Spouses: Forgive, love and respect them. Take specific actions (e.g., buy flowers, clean, compliment, etc.) to show respect and love.

5. Children: Realize the child is a teacher, showing you that what matters in life is not so much you, but the other.

6. Friends: Cultivate true friends, ones whom you love without an expectation of receiving anything in return. And realize you will become like the friends you choose, so choose wisely.

FIVE

Live in the Present.

There is only one time that is important — NOW! It is the most important time because it is the only time that we have any power.
— Leo Tolstoy

Remember, today is the tomorrow you worried about yesterday.
— Dale Carnegie

S top.
That's one thing we find difficult to do in the modern world. Life just keeps getting faster and faster. Think about it. It was only 100 years ago when most people used horses or sailed from place to place. No TV or radio, few distractions, just time to think and be with yourself.

Now everything operates at a super accelerated rate. We hurtle through the sky from continent to continent in pursuit of careers and money. We juggle cell phones, PDAs and laptops, responding to beeps and alerts like some lab monkey. We punch through hundreds of emails a day, when our father's father got one letter a month. And life will only get faster and faster.

This is hardly a new observation. But while people may know things are moving at a faster rate, they are more and more caught up in it, unable to slow it down. Even worse, our minds are racing too. We've gotten so much in the habit of going, we can't stop. We can't slow down. We let the whirlwind just take us around and around.

We can't just *be* in the moment.

This is another fundamental obstacle to happiness in the modern world: we aren't living in the moment. We spend too much thinking — some of us even obsessing about ourselves. We are restless and anxious — reliving the past or worrying about the future. We are constantly seeking distraction from our current condition, watching TV, wearing headphones, playing video games, etc. We are living elsewhere, detached from ourselves. It is almost as if we are watching our life as a movie. Things happen to us, but we aren't really there.

One thing is certain, we are not mindfully appreciating the here and now. The moment. And that, unfortunately, is where life happens — in the moment. It's where happiness is hiding.

 ## Your Brain Runs Free

What do I mean when I say our minds are racing? Pause for a minute and think about how your brain operates from moment to moment from the point you wake up in the morning. If it's like most peoples' brains it begins operating as if independent of yourself, you are like a spectator watching these thoughts stream by. One thought ends as another pushes in. Your brain takes off and doesn't stop until your head hits the pillow in the evening.

These thoughts can be extremely vivid. In fact, many of them appear like your own personal video recordings. It is like you're watching little movie clips of your life, past and future. You've stored a whole library of videos about your experiences, relationships, hopes and fears. Your brain kicks off and randomly plays these clips like some video juke box player.

Each one of these thoughts is accompanied by a related emotion. From that moment you wake up and get in the shower, your video library kicks off. You are being buffeted by emotions around these images: that image in the mirror that you caught of your expanding belly, the day at school you were humiliated, how someone at the office got the promotion you deserved, how your spouse spent too much yesterday, or how your parents were unfair with you. The images also review what will happen today, whether you will be nervous in today's presentation, whether you will get a raise today, or whether your child will behave at the store.

Not all the thoughts have to be negative or worrying, though many of them are. The point is that it is exhausting to go through all these videos and their related emotions. You are up and down in minutes or seconds, buffeted about by the random workings of these images. And since most of these revolve around a personal critique of your life, they are an assault on yourself and your ability to love yourself. That's why tens of millions of us are popping depression and anti-anxiety pills. These pills chemically slow you down. They chemically tell the brain to stop jumping about, forcing it to be in the moment.

A Habit of Chaos

Let's spend a little more time looking at where our brains typically take us. This will help us recognize when these little video brain trips begin and to become better at interrupting them to stay in the present, in the moment.

Usually your brain avoids the present by taking you to the past or the future. If we go back to your morning shower, instead of enjoying moment in the water, you are fixating on something else. We tend to be pretty tough on ourselves. Reviewing how we might have failed in the past or worrying about obstacles in the future.

As we'll review in Key Seven: "Love Yourself," your difficulty in loving yourself stems in large part from how you think you are judged.

> *We juggle cell phones, PDAs and laptops, responding to beeps and alerts like some lab monkey.*

These messages get programmed into you — they help create your video library. Maybe your father told you would not amount to anything. Maybe a teacher called you stupid. Or maybe some kids said you were fat.

You have developed life long habits of repeating these lectures, statements and videotapes reviewing your failings. If your in that shower thinking about something negative, studies show you can repeat that statement to yourself more than 600 times that day. Could any person survive such an assault with a healthy view of the self? No.

So there you are. Living your life, day-in-and-day-out at the whim of where your brain takes you. Finding a moment of quiet and solitude where we just live in the moment is very rare. The really startling thing is that even if the opportunity for such a moment arises, we have developed an endless number of distractions to ensure that we never have to live in the moment.

Think about it. As soon as we have a moment to be with ourselves, we turn on the TV or radio. In recent years, video games have also become a mind-numbing distraction. And with the popularity of portable music players, few people take walks or go to the gym without their eardrums throbbing. Or think about how music videos and movies now cut from scene-to-scene amid pounding music, giving you no time to pause and reflect.

It is clear why these distractions have become popular. They do have the effect of interrupting the brain and shutting down the video library.

That is not to say that all distractions are bad all the time. Rather we just need to become aware of what we are doing. Don't let your mind hop around all day and then plop in front of the TV to interrupt it. Gain control of your brain and, after that, you can watch TV or listen to the radio — but be mindful of living in the moment.

No Pause, No Happiness

Why does any of this matter? How is it connected to your happiness? As we've reviewed, happiness happens in the moment and if you aren't living in the here and now — if you're in the past or future — you are missing life as it happens. If your mind is unquiet, you will remain buffeted about by whatever winds prevail that day. It is stress and anxiety driven. It is the exact opposite of well-being.

So how do we get better control of our brains and learn to spend more time in the moment? It takes practice. Again, you are replacing bad habits with good habits. So it also takes time.

One thing you can do is to remind yourself of the moment you are in. Hopefully, you can tell yourself how joyful it is to be in this moment. Every time thoughts begin to carry you away or a video starts playing, shut them down. Remind yourself to stay in the here and now. Turn off the cell phone, PDA and laptop. Put them away on weekends.

Another thing you can do is pause. Physically stop throughout the day. Sit down on a park bench, breathe quietly, look at the swaying trees or rippling water, and slowly push the thoughts away. Take a walk — in nature if you can — focus your eyes on things, chase the thoughts away, breathe quietly and slow your brain down. Look at a picture of a loved one on your desk, smile slightly, breathe, focus and relax. Make up your own daily "pauses." And place reminders on your mirrors, refrigerators, TVs, car radios and computers, which remind you to pause.

Another thing you can do is just breathe. Take a deep breathe. As you inhale, forcefully push your belly out first, filling the lower part of your lungs. Keep inhaling as you now expand your chest. Envision the air flowing to the outer reaches of your hands and feet. Now reverse. Expel the breathe from the diaphragm level as the belly contracts and then push the breathe out of the chest. That is a full breathe. We spend all of our lives taking half or third breathes. Enjoy a full breath and think about it as the air moves in and out.

If you want to take it to the next step, do a mini-meditation. This is probably the most effective means to retraining your brain to spend more time locked on the present. Why is this necessary? Your brain has learned deeply engrained habits and it will repeat them unless you create some new habits.

Studies show that meditation effectively slows down different parts of the brain, including the frontal lobe, the part of the brain responsible for emotions, reasoning and self-conscious awareness. In fact, one study showed how an area of the brain connected with negative thoughts was slowed. It is what Buddhists call becoming mindful. You can also see that some Christians who pray very deeply achieve similar results.

And if you want to give it a shot, try meditating. But whether you meditate or not is, obviously, entirely up to you. The point is to try to get better at slowing your brain down and living in the moment. Meditation is just one technique. For religious people, deep prayer can have a similar effect.

Another helpful tactic is to consider why you are so distracted. A good part of it results from the goals you have chosen to pursue. As we'll see in the next section, many of those objectives have no correlation to your happiness. You could be, for example, running from appointment to appointment only to acquire things that are not important to

How to Meditate

To mediate, try the following: Sit on a chair or on the floor (possibly on top of a pillow). Place your right hand palm up in your lap and put your left hand palm up on top of it. Avoid bright lights. Keep your eyes open and unfocused. Use the breathing technique described above. Inhale slowly and count that as one. Exhale slowly and count that as two. Go to ten and start again. Do it for 5 minutes. Set a timer. Doing this once in the morning and once in the evening is best. Focus on the breathing. As thoughts stream in, gently push them out. Try to clear the mind of everything but the breathing and counting. It's very difficult, but concentrate on the counting and over time you will get good at it. You will have succeeded when you sit for 20 or 30 minutes and have totally cleared your mind.

you. You should evaluate your life and its pace and determine if the price you are paying is worth it. We examined this more in the last key.

It also helps to realize that one of the fundamental causes of your racing brain is your fear of not controlling your life — which we covered somewhat in Key Two: "Choose Real Freedom." Suffice it to say now that you will spend less time dwelling on your past failings and your future worries if you just learn to genuinely accept that you are not in control. Nobody is. Life happens and we can only do our best. A true acceptance of just trying to do your best will be extremely freeing. It will allow you to release the past and the future, to live in the moment and be more content, quiet and, hopefully, happy.

Appreciate every second of the moment that is happening. Practice it and it will become a habit.

In Review

1. Realize that your brain buffets you to and fro. And you let it.
2. Stop distracting yourself with the TV, radio, videogames, etc. Pause and reflect.
3. Take Action: Interrupt your brain and teach it new habits:
    a. Strategically place reminders to pause and be in the moment.
    b. Try sitting on a park bench, looking out the window; etc.
    c. Try meditating or deep prayer.
4. Live in the present.

SIX

Be Virtuous.

Happiness is the highest good, [and it comes from the] perfect practice of virtue, which some can attain, while others have little or none of it.

— Aristotle

Men are equal; it is not birth but virtue that makes the difference.

— Voltaire

It's what you've always been taught. Be a good person. Do the right thing. Be virtuous.

It kind of makes sense. If your goal is to be happy, look around. The people behaving badly do not tend to be very happy. Those taking drugs, especially to excess, are certainly unhappy. Those stealing things or breaking the law, end up with troubled lives. Or those that mistreat others are often bitter themselves.

But if you're like most people while you were growing up, when you asked, "Why should I be good? Why can't I hit Johnny?" The cliché response was: "Because you shouldn't." Or: "It's not nice." Or: "It's wrong."

Nobody probably sat you down at that young age and tried to explain to you that there is a strong link between your happiness and being virtuous. So you went through your life like most people, behaving in a fairly decent manner because you were taught to. Maybe you learned the "Golden Rule" about treating others as you wish to be treated and it made sense. You formed some habits of behaving well. And that is perfectly fine. As the Greek philosophers taught, that is what a good society or culture is supposed to do, teach the citizens how to behave so that they might have a more fulfilling life. Ultimately, the Greeks taught it was our nature to be good and feel bad when we are not.

You can sustain a fairly happy existence just doing what you were taught — presuming you had good teachers, e.g., parents, friends, etc. This is true even if you are completely oblivious to the reasons you are behaving as you do — even if the only reason you behave morally is because that is what people expect of you.

But you can certainly achieve a more content life by better understanding the link between virtue and happiness. When we know the reasons why we need to behave in a certain manner it can sometimes make it easier, even enjoyable.

Making Right Choices

Being virtuous and being happy are really about making the right choices, the choices that are good for you. Sure, that sounds easy, but how can you know what choices are the "right"? The Greek philosopher, Aristotle, once explained: The right choices are those that are in line with our nature.

OK. What does that mean? Quite simply human beings are born wanting to be happy. Do you want to be miserable? No. Well, in order to be happy, you need to listen to your in-born nature. And our human nature demands that we be virtuous.

By following these guideposts to behavior you make good choices, choices that carry you in the direction of happiness and away from being miserable. After you've made many correct choices you form a habit of choosing well. It should become unpleasant for you act against your habits — because you're acting in a manner that is against your nature and one that postpones happiness.

Test this theory. See if you will be happy if you start doing bad or nasty things. You can also get some indication that being virtuous leads to happiness because many cultures around the world support this notion as it's been proven over thousands of years.

> '*When I do good, I feel good. When I do bad, I feel bad. That is my religion.*'
> — ABRAHAM LINCOLN

Abraham Lincoln summed it up nicely: "When I do good, I feel good. When I do bad, I feel bad. That is my religion."

Some examples will help explain this.

A young man confronted Plato and told him that the best policy was to try to have power over others and then you could impose your will and be happy. Plato showed that if that person could rule over others, eventually he would grow paranoid and obsessed with maintaining his power. He would, in short, be unhappy. He further showed that this was not aligned with man's true nature, to be good, to be virtuous.

ARISTOTLE SHOWS THE WAY

To help guide us, Aristotle actually listed out some key virtues. By following these and acting upon them, you will be laying the foundation for a happy life. One of Aristotle's key pieces of advice in following these virtues was to do everything in moderation. Seek a balance in each virtue — and we'll review specific examples in a minute.

Let's now look at some specific examples of virtues that Aristotle listed and how they are intertwined with achieving a happy life:

- You should have *self-control*. That is just another way of telling you that should not be tempted to overindulge in pleasurable things. We all love pleasure: good food, lying on the couch, sex, watching our favorite show, etc. The key is indulging in these things in the right amount. You need to recognize that short-term pleasures are often at odds with achieving a more happy life. Think about food. If you love to eat, you probably eat too much. And just as we discussed earlier, you need to acknowledge that the short-term pleasure of popping that bon bon in your mouth is followed by a long term unhappiness of being overweight. You shouldn't over-indulge pleasures, or, for that matter, under-indulge. You need to find the right balance.

- You need to be *courageous*. This does not mean you need to join the army and become a hero. You can show courage in all aspects of your life. Courage is a developed habit of being able to face down some fear or endure some pain for a greater good. You may need to pay some price to stand up to injustice, such as standing up to a bully. Or you may need to face the pain of exercising to lose weight. You need to undergo the hardship of studying to graduate from school. If you don't, that is a form of cowardice. Start with small things and build up. Conquer fears and promote your confidence to go and do what you thought impossible.

  And again, you need to be courageous in a balanced way. You don't want to be rash — accepting certain death to save a dog — and you don't want to be a coward either — running away from every confrontation. You need to conquer fear and take chances. Courage comes from practice. Take small steps and over the months and years you will find yourself having more of it.

- You should be *generous*. Giving is a way of expressing your love and concern for others. And as we've seen, your ability to love others is integrally connected to your chances of finding happiness. But again, you need to be charitable in a balanced manner. You don't want to be stingy and mean — not reaching out or giving to others — just as you shouldn't be excessive and wasteful — donating so much that you can't live yourself. Find a balance. Just do it without any expectation of return. Do it quietly. Don't announce your actions. Do the things for their own sake.

- You need *pride*. This is often considered a dirty word in our society. It implies you are an egoist. Christians rightfully consider pride a sin. But the sin is really in an excess of pride. You shouldn't be vain and self-centered. Nor should you be so humble that you let others step all over you. Pride is very important to your dignity and your ability to love yourself — a key element of happiness as we will discuss. If you don't believe in yourself, little else is possible. And if you are full of yourself, you are probably a weak and scared person — someone who also has a hard time loving himself or herself. Have pride, but in moderation. This is a tough one. Ben Franklin said that humility was one of his toughest battles.

- You should develop a *good temper*. You've often heard the phrase: "He has a bad temper." Well that's just what you don't want. Having a good temper merely means that you approach life on an even keel. You have a fair and just way of responding to situations. So when your spouse spends too much money, you shouldn't being throwing pots around the house. That doesn't mean you should walk around all day just smiling, not responding to anything. You should occasionally get angry. Just get angry in the right situations. If someone is trying to hurt you, you should obviously respond. If you're angry all the time or if you are letting people walk all over you, you've obviously strayed from the path of happiness. Again, it is just a question of balance.

- You must be *friendly*. This seems obvious, and it should. But this is more than just being nice. It is actually a virtue to develop and maintain good friends. In fact, it is one of the most important virtues — as we discussed Key Three: "Cherish Friends and Family." The most important point is that in order to be happy, you need friends. We are social creatures. And in order to win and keep good friends, you need to behave well. You need to be loyal, kind, giving, civil, sincere, reasonable, loving, truthful and just — to name a few.

  Choose your friends carefully because you will become like those you are around. This is why making the right choices is so critically linked to happiness. Of course, you don't want to act as though no one is good enough for you. And on the other hand you don't want to be too friendly. If you just randomly give your friendship away, it probably doesn't mean that much. And worse, you are probably associating with people you probably shouldn't.

- You need to be *truthful*. This may sound like your first grade teacher, but don't underestimate the power of being honest. You cannot maintain your dignity and lie. Truthfulness includes being honest with yourself. If you cannot accurately assess your life and your relationships, you cannot improve your situation. If your life is a mess or if you are being a bit of a jerk to those around you, you'll never find the path to happiness until you confront yourself with the facts. And if you aren't honest to those around you, you are violating their trust. You are failing to love them. You are failing to respect yourself. And you are failing to live happily.

- Have some sense of *modesty*. This is really that little voice in your head that's telling you shouldn't be running down the street naked. But modesty also points us toward happiness in more subtle ways. It makes you feel guilty when you do eat that bonbon. It tells you that should have studied harder for the test. It is kind of an internal regulator that keeps you from overindulging things or failing to behave as you should. It should stop you from being to vain, or trying to be everyone's friend, or from lying, or not giving anything to a needy person. On the other hand, don't waste your time feeling excessive guilt. That is also a sure recipe for unhappiness. Regulate yourself. If you are feeling too little or too much shame, tell yourself and correct the situation. We're all human, we make mistakes.

- You must be *just* or *fair-minded*. This is one of the most important virtues. You must treat others fairly and with justice. If you are not, it is the clearest sign that you have no love or respect for them. If you do not respect others, you cannot respect yourself. Justice is a very difficult concept and cannot easily be outlined here. But suffice it to say that we all need to strive for it.

Each one of these virtues could be a book by themselves. The key here is to provide you with a few high level guideposts to help you on the road to happiness. All of these virtues, if practiced, will make you a happier person, because it is your nature to want to act in accordance with these moral goals. Try acting against them and you'll see the result. Eat all you want. Hit someone for no reason. Start being extremely arrogant about your accomplishments. You will not be happy. And if that's the case, try the opposite of each one of those.

The Joy of Virtues

You shouldn't feel, like your parents told you, that you *have* to be virtuous, that it's a burden that we have to fulfill. If you understand virtue and its connection to your happiness, you will *want* to be virtuous. The fact is we grow up believing that we'd prefer to eat bonbons and have sex when and with whom we desire. We think that being virtuous means denying ourselves all these things that give us pleasure. In other words, it's painful to be virtuous. Why shouldn't I eat what I want, fill the house with electronic toys, buy four cars and vacation in Italy?

Go ahead. But what you should remember is that pleasure does not equal happiness. And once you understand that, you realize that virtue is not about denying yourself something. It is about following the only authentic path to happiness. By putting that bonbon away, going to the gym, you are proclaiming that you want to be happy. And with that recognition you should *want* to be virtuous. You will even learn to take pleasure in being virtuous and denying your desires because you know in your heart you are a happier person because of it. The alternative is to chase the false gods of happiness: food, appearances, things, sex, leisure, etc. It is all vanity and foolishness.

You Are What You Do

One final but key point that is easily overlooked is that all this discussion about virtue is just that: Talk! Virtue on the other hand is all about action. If you are sitting in room all your life thinking moral thoughts, it doesn't mean that you are virtuous or happy. You need to get out there and practice these virtues.

It is through this constant practice that you develop new habits to replace your old habits. You develop, as Aristotle described, a disposition or character that tells you to do the right thing. You shouldn't really have to think about whether you should be courageous or not. Your disposition, having been trained over the years, will reflexively help you act in the correct manner. Your feelings don't just happen — they come from your character that was hopefully well crafted over the years.

So, in other words, when you feel sorry for yourself, feel like running away from situations you shouldn't, feel like throwing a temper tantrum, feel no shame when you should, etc., you've learned this behavior. Your task is to change that, to change your disposition. You do this, as we've said, through practicing the virtues listed above.

And remember our concert violinist in the introduction? She didn't get to the concert hall just by thinking about being a star and hearing applause. She had to focus on how to play the violin better. She worked eight hours day and skipped vacations. It is the same with virtue. Don't fixate on the happiness virtue might bring. If you do that you'll be focused on the goal too much and forget the work. You need to focus on developing new habits of virtue and the happiness it brings is a by-product. That's because you should do virtuous things for their own sake, not because you greedily want them to produce a happy life for yourself — if that's the case, you have the wrong intent.

To sum up: Try to be a gentleman or gentlewoman. This person is always concerned with the feelings and thoughts of those next to them. If you are working to make them comfortable and happy, you are caring for both of you. This person is not arrogant, but quietly confident. They are courageous and just. They see that many virtues live in small gestures, a kind word or a helping hand. Become this person and you will be happier.

Only through your actions can you be virtuous. And only through your behavior can you be happy.

In Review

1. Doing good brings happiness.
2. Memorize these virtues and practice them. Post them on your mirror or computer.
   a. Have self-control.
   b. Be courageous.
   c. Be generous.
   d. Have pride.
   e. Have a good temper.
   f. Be friendly.
   g. Be truthful.
   h. Be modest.
   i. Be just.
3. Do these things for their own sake, not to impress yourself or others.
4. Take action: Learn new habits by acting on A-I above repeatedly.

SEVEN

Love Yourself.

Self-love is an instrument useful but dangerous: it often wounds the hand which makes use of it, and seldom does good without doing harm.
— ROUSSEAU

Two of the most difficult but important keys come at the end: love yourself and love others.

First, to be happy, you must love yourself, properly.

But if you're like most people you think more about loving others than yourself. Most of us don't go around thinking: "Gee, you know, I really loved myself today." That can sound odd or even vain.

The fact is that proper self-love is a fundamental ingredient of genuine happiness, a life-long sense of well being that comes from a deep acceptance, forgiveness and respect of the self. This acceptance of yourself infuses you with a profound sense of well-being. If you're wondering why this is important, consider the alternative.

And before we continue, just a point of clarification. We are not talking about providing yet another means of pumping up your self-esteem or encouraging some narcissistic behavior. We are talking about — as we shall see — encouraging a quiet acceptance of yourself.

So how do you achieve this? As the philosopher Rousseau taught, there is a right way and wrong way to love yourself. Most of us go about it all wrong. So first let's look at what we tend to do, and then what we should do.

The Wrong Approach

In our busy day-to-day lives, most of us don't tend to take the time to learn how we can get better at loving ourselves — by forgiving, accepting and respecting ourselves more. Instead, we live distracted lives, constantly thinking about family affairs, office conflicts, relationship issues, etc. Our minds bounce from one situation to the next until our head hits the pillow.

Throughout the busy day, if you're like most of us, you tend to engage in frequent internal dialogues about how you *feel* about yourself in the moment. This is the wrong approach. What does that mean? Let's review what you do.

You engage in some internal dialogues that are negative, you think: "I'm overweight." "I'm an idiot." "I looked nervous at the meeting." "She (or he) won't go out with me." "My joke didn't work, I feel like a fool." "My career is in a stall." Other people often prompt these statements, but you are really the expert at putting yourself down — engaging in self-criticism or even self-hatred.

Then you engage in some internal daily dialogues that are positive, you think: "I really do have an impressive job." "I am pretty wealthy." "I am smarter than these people." "I really am pretty good looking." "I do have a fair amount of power." If you spend too much time thinking this way, you are vain.

If you're like most of us, you spend the day engaging in both kinds of dialogues. It's like the stock market: up and down. You are *pleased* with yourself or you're not depending on what happened that day, which is vain and silly.

But the key point here is that both these negative and positive judgments have got you thinking about yourself in the wrong way. You think that if you just maximize the positive judgments and minimize the negative ones, then you'll love yourself more. But you need to realize that when you are judged (positively or negatively), it is because you are either meeting or failing to live up to the expectations that you and others have set. And the vast majority of times, these are superficial expectations about whether you are wealthy, beautiful, witty, famous, powerful, or whatever. None of these things, as we've reviewed, are required for you to love yourself or to make you happy. If you were to have one more day to live, would any of these things be important? No. So why are you letting them ruin your life?

A German philosopher once said, other peoples' heads are a horrible place to live.

Yet, we beat ourselves up. As noted, studies show that we can repeat a negative thought as many as 600 times a day. And if we are putting ourselves down, you can bet we let others do it also. As a wise German philosopher, Schopenhauer, once said: Other peoples' heads are horrible place to live. Dale Carnegie also put it well: "Did you ever see an unhappy horse? Did you ever see bird that had the blues? One reason why birds and horses are not unhappy is because they are not trying to impress other birds and horses."

Obviously, sometimes you deserve criticism — from yourself and others — especially if you're acting cruel, lazy, unloving, cowardly, hostile, etc. The key is to become aware of your thinking, accepting legitimate criticism and rejecting the superficial.

At this point we could get into the origin of all this mental baggage.

But unless you are that *especially* rare case that has experienced severe physically or mentally abuse, there is only one message: Get over it. Life is difficult. Stop these thoughts. Dump this bad habit for some new ones. How? Read on.

The Right Approach

We've reviewed the wrong way to love yourself. So what's the right way? How can you stop focusing on superficial judgments about yourself and learn proper self-love?

Our Greek philosopher, Aristotle, provides a simple principle to guide you: Always *love yourself as you would your best friend.* Just as you would with a special friend, you should judge yourself fairly, be honest with yourself, respect yourself, forgive yourself and be good to yourself.

Let's look at each of these individually:

Think about how you judge your real friends and then ask if you judge yourself in a similar way. Would you tell your best friend that she is fat, ugly, dull, slow and poor? No, you wouldn't. So why do you say those things to yourself? Even if she is all those things, they are irrelevant. You are friends and you love her for other reasons: you share an interest, a sense of humor, a way of looking at the world, etc. And if she happened to be beautiful, thin, smart, exciting and rich, you wouldn't just blurt out to her that these are the reasons you're her friend and you love her. These things are irrelevant. If those are the reasons you are friends, she is not a real friend. Judge friends on whether they are good people. Judge yourself in a similar manner.

Friends are also *honest* with each other. So be honest with yourself. It's a key element of learning to love yourself. Stop trying to be someone you are not. Stop fooling yourself that beauty, power, wittiness, fame, money, or whatever are important and will make you love yourself or bring you happiness. When you aren't trying to live up to superficial expectations, when you behave in a manner that is in sync with whom you really are, you are on the road to being authentic. Tension, fear and insecurity come from being something you are not. After all, you might be found out! Mahatma Gandhi, the Indian leader and philosopher, said it best: *"Happiness is when what you think, what you say, and what you do are in harmony."* You are happy if you are authentic — in other words, honest with whom you are.

Respect is a critical part of any friendship and so to should you *respect* yourself. You cannot love yourself without some self-respect. If you do not respect yourself, you show it. You abuse yourself in public and in private. You put yourself down. You eat too much. You don't take on challenges — after all how could someone as lowly as you succeed? You let others push you aside. So you must nurture your inherent dignity. All humans have a strong natural dignity. If you let it get corroded away by superficial judgments about whether you are pretty or rich, then you aren't respecting yourself. More importantly, you are making it very difficult to love yourself.

A key part of any friendship is *forgiveness*. So you must forgive yourself to love yourself. Every time you reflexively begin to engage in superficial self-criticism or self-loathing, shake your head, and say aloud, "Stop it." Forgive yourself. Every time you reflexively feel self-satisfied because of a superficial source of self-esteem (e.g., appearances, jobs, money, etc.), laugh and forgive yourself for being a fool. Genuine happiness, life-long happiness, comes from a deep and willful acceptance and forgiveness of yourself.

Finally, friendship requires that you are *good* to the other person. What does it mean to be good to yourself? It doesn't mean getting to eat an extra piece of cake. Here, good means whether you are treating yourself well — as a person with dignity should be treated. Are you being fair with yourself? Are you being honest? Are you being modest?

In other words, are you harming yourself by shamelessly sleeping with anything that breaths? Do you have a sense of pride (but not too much)? Do you stand up for yourself (in a courageous way)? Are your emotions in balance? In other words, do you have a good temperament?

All these questions, believe it or not, are asking whether you are virtuous toward yourself and others. We learned more about this in Key Six: "Be Virtuous." In short, just try acting like the opposite of the virtues listed in Key Six: Be a hot-head, unfair, a coward, without shame, without self-control, and cheap. You will be unhappy because this is just another way injuring your dignity, of telling yourself you aren't worthy. You'll be acting against your nature. You'll be unbalanced and unhappy.

One last, but very important point, is that all love, including self-love is really about *action*. Love is not about sitting in a room and thinking about yourself. It is about the things you do to and for yourself. In other words, if you are honest, respectful, forgiving and good toward yourself, it means these things will change your behavior. For example, if you are honest with yourself, you may need to change careers. If you are going to respect yourself, you will need to stop eating so much. And if you are going to forgive yourself, you'll need to stop those superficial self-critical statements. If you are good to yourself, you will need to stand up for yourself when someone is putting you down.

Learn New Habits

You are your habits (which are really just actions that you tend to repeat). So end the habits that harm you and engage in the habits that promote proper self-love. We'll learn more about this in Key 10: "Take Action."

Only once you love yourself will you have the confidence to fulfill the rest of these keys. You can't really love others until you love yourself. You can't live in the present, if you are constantly focused on how you messed up your past or will screw up your future. You can't pursue your true calling unless you are honest with yourself. And so on.

This is the most difficult key to understand and act on. But by acting on the other keys here you will also be working toward a greater self-love.

In Review

1. Loving yourself is a key ingredient to happiness.
2. The wrong approach to loving yourself means you are pleased or displeased with yourself based on superficial judgments about whether you are attractive, rich, smart, popular, famous, etc.
3. The right approach means that you love yourself as you would your best friend:
    a. Be honest with yourself.
    b. Respect yourself.
    c. Forgive yourself.
    d. Be good (virtuous) to yourself.
4. Take action. Stop doing #2 and start doing #3.

EIGHT
Love Others.

*One word frees us of all the weight and pain of life:
That word is love.*

— Sophocles

To be happy, you must love others.

It's pretty obvious why this is a requirement of happiness. If you loved no one and no one loved you, would be alone. And it is your human nature to want to be in a group, maintain relations and love. Rejecting this is to ignore what Aristotle described as your pre-programmed nature to be a social animal. You would not be true to yourself and, worse, you would not be happy.

The Wrong Approach

Before we cover what it means to love others, let's pause and review how some of us tend to go about this in the wrong way — just as we do when we are trying to love ourselves.

Think about someone you "love." Most of us tend to take that word for granted. It is kind of a vague thing anyway. What does it mean to love another? Is it the way you sign a letter? A hug at the door? A warm thought? Many of us would say, "Sure, I love _____." But the fact is that we don't spend much time thinking about what it means or how it should change our behavior.

On a day-to-day basis many of us think less in terms of whether we love others and more about whether we are getting along with them. Think about some of those close to you. Think of the battles you've had with your parents. How they wronged you. Think of how your spouse doesn't seem to contribute as much as you. Maybe he won't clean the kitchen or she won't stop spending money. Think how your siblings never quite see things from your perspective or how they might have been the parents' favorite. Think of how a boyfriend or girlfriend is not as considerate as you. Think of how your children don't seem to love you as they once did, unconditionally and full of innocence. Maybe they hurt you by not reciprocating your love or by saying harmful things. And to track all these slights and hurts, some of us even keep mental scorecards.

> *A complicating factor in our ability to love relates back to whether we love ourselves.*

The bottom line is that we are typically willing to love those around us if they live up to *our* expectations and behave well toward us. If we feel that they accept us and that they act fairly toward us, then we return the favor. This shouldn't be a surprise as we are all insecure to some degree, so we fear reaching out and facing rejection. We fear being judged negatively. We want acceptance. And we read rejection into the smallest details of life, feeling betrayed if a spouse doesn't compliment us, if a friend doesn't return a favor, if a parent is unfair, etc.

What complicates this picture is that we are caught up in our mundane (and very often petty) day-to-day issues of work, chores, social obligations, etc. When those around don't fall into line and appreciate our perspective or pain, many of us react negatively. We feel we've been wronged and are owed something.

The result is that we protect ourselves. We steel ourselves against the world. We do this by handing out a kind of *conditional* love: "If they accept and love me, I will do the same. But I will keep monitoring the situation for any change." This kind of love is stingily returned by those closest to us, so we go to sleep wounded. Some of us even harbor a quiet or not-so-quiet anger.

And we're talking about the people close to you! Think how much more difficult it is to love strangers or those who need your help. We can't seem to love our own relations at the level we should because they didn't take out the trash. But then think about Pope John Paul II, who absolutely forgave and loved his attempted assassin. That tells you there's room for improvement.

Of course, we love those close to us, but because of the injuries they inflict, and our conscious and subconscious scorecards, we don't love them as we should — at a higher, or more *unconditional,* level.

Time goes by. Sometimes the ones we try to love leave or die and suddenly we regret the lost opportunity. We focused on the pettiness and forgot the fundamentals.

The Right Approach

So what can we do to learn to love others better?

It's not easy, but we already have a starting point because loving others is very much like loving yourself. To love others you must be honest, forgiving, accepting, respectful and good — just as you must be toward yourself. Go back to the end of the previous section and think about how you can apply those principles to others — and we'll circle back to them at the end of this key.

In the last key we also said that you should treat yourself like your best friend. Here, we're reviewing a little bit more about how you should treat your best friends, and others.

Examples are always helpful, especially with ambiguous ideas like love. So let's review some real life examples of real people who are great at loving others. Think about someone you've met that more than anything else *is* love. They accept, respect, forgive and love those around them. Maybe you had a grandparent like this. But unless you know someone very special, it is not likely that you come into daily contact with a person who is loving in nearly all they do. That's a rare bird.

Beyond those close to you, think about those, living and dead, who embody love: Pope John Paul II, the Dalai Lama, Mother Theresa, Jesus, and Buddha. We admire them. We try to be more like them. Why? They have what we long for. They are love. And we know instinctively, by our natures, that love is a key to our happiness.

But why do they embody love? What do they do? If you were to sum it all up, you'd say that they exist for others. They accept the other. And they demonstrate this every day in every moment with actions. The key to understanding them is that love is not some intellectual exercise, it is action.

Think of those who embody love. Think of Mother Theresa attending to the poorest of the poor, putting bandages on the open sores of leprosy patients. Think of Pope John Paul II visiting his would-be assassin in prison, and taking his head in his hands to forgive him. Think of the Dalai Lama who teaches love even as the Chinese government tortures and kills his people.

All these people love unconditionally — or come close. They respect the dignity of each human life. They give. They forgive and they accept those that come before them. You might think the only way to do that is to suspend judgment, to not condemn others for their actions — for harmful behavior, for example. But that's wrong. Pope John Paul II did and the Dalai Lama does judge people. But the key question is what do they judge people for? And what is their response to this judgment? At a fundamental level, they judge people on whether they are loving. They condemn acts that are not loving.

But in doing so, they simultaneously acknowledge the frailty and fallen nature of man. And all at once they forgive and even grieve for the one doing harm, because he is more lost than the person receiving his blows. That is why Pope John Paul II can condemn his assassin's actions but forgive the man — even pray for the man, because he is further from love and deeper in pain than anyone. Pope John Paul II's would-be assassin said the forgiveness he received in prison was "the most beautiful, the most significant moment" of his life.

How Do We Compare?

Now compare those that embody love to ourselves. How do we compare? We don't. Certainly we try. But we fail. We fail not only in loving those who harm us, but in loving those who love us!

Why is that? Again, it comes back to *judgment*. We make very different kinds of judgments about those around us than these leaders of love do.

Consider your reaction when you feel injured by another. Now think about when those that embody love are injured by or displeased with those around them. It does not interfere with their ability to give, respect, forgive, accept and love. We on the other hand are different animals. When we're injured, many of us log it in our elephant memory bank. Others may forgive, but it is not an absolute forgiveness.

Love Yourself, Then Others

A real complicating factor in our ability to forgive and love more completely relates back to whether we love ourselves. If you are not very comfortable, accepting, respecting, forgiving and loving yourself, you won't be with others either. Loving others is difficult when you are busy hating yourself over petty issues: lacking looks, being overweight, not being liked, etc. Because you spend so much time beating yourself up, you are only that much more sensitive when those around you don't give you love and support. It is a nasty spiral. The more you're down on yourself, the less able you are to love others. And that makes it more difficult for others to love you, which only makes you feel more worthless.

Do you think the Dalai Lama is or Pope John Paul II was consumed with how they looked on any given day? In their lives, they weren't concerned with IQ, money, power and fame. They rejected that world. They knew that true happiness comes from unconditional love. They knew that love grew from within. It grew from a calm and assured acceptance and respect of themselves — that they were good people. They were secure in themselves. This security allows them to love.

At the same time, they are humans who fail and need forgiveness. Knowing their fallibility they can turn to those in the world and recognize they too are fallen. That people need forgiveness, respect, acceptance and love just like themselves. And they know that the more they love, the more they are loved.

Of course, knowing and doing are two different things. In a certain sense it was easier for Pope John Paul II and the Dalai Lama because they devoted their life to prayer, meditation, contemplation and love. We have to run around and earn a living. It almost seems like we don't have time to love.

Action Items

So what specific things can you do?

First, *love yourself.* You can't love others until you are comfortable in your own skin. Accept, respect, forgive and be good to yourself and then to those around you. See the Key Seven: "Love Yourself" and Key Four: "Cherish Family and Friends" for more details.

Second, take Aristotle's and Christ's advice and *treat others as you treat yourself* — or perhaps even better, if you tend to beat yourself up. Be fair, honest, forgiving and virtuous. This Golden Rule behavior is also something the latest genetics studies show is encoded into our being. We are reciprocally altruistic creatures.

Third, take action, because *love is action.* Accepting, respecting, forgiving and being good to others are actions. Compliment someone. Tell them you love them "no matter what." Clean the house. Buy flowers. Work in a soup kitchen. And try this trick: Don't tell anyone. Do these acts for their own sake, not for winning favorable judgments from others. All these actions are really about treating others well. Learn these new habits. We'll go over more about this behavior in Key Six: "Be Virtuous."

Fourth, *have patience.* It takes times to replace bad habits with good ones. You've spent a lifetime developing your reactions, your temper, your slowness to forgive, and your unwillingness to accept all with open arms. Don't kid yourself, you have room for improvement. But you need time to deconstruct these habits and replace them with new ones.

Fifth, *empathize with others.* Think about the pain others feel. It may be causing those close to you to lash out at you. Their rejection of you may have more to do with themselves than with you. From the janitor to the Wall Street banker, everyone has hidden insecurities, rejections and pain. In fact, you should empathize most with that banker, because he is the one that will most likely chase that dollar into the grave — and never find happiness.

Sixth, review your relationships — the entire history of each one. *Forgive* all those who transgressed against you. Move on. Period.

Seventh, go about giving and loving with an expectation that others may not reciprocate. This is not a test to see whether others will return your love, this is a test to see whether *you* can love. Loving is not about whether you get something in return. In other words, *don't make your love conditional.*

Eighth, see the big picture. *Life is short.* Do you want to be consumed with your petty scorecards on what people did to you or how you've been wronged? Or do you want to love and be happy?

Finally, acknowledge you're human. *You are going to fail at this.* That is not the point. Only a perfect person avoids failure. And there are no perfect people. The point is to try, to fail, and try again. That is the entire point of life. If you try hard, you may get closer to the levels of those who embody love. And that is true happiness.

In Review

1. Loving others is a key to your happiness.
2. Don't make your love of others conditional on how you are treated.
3. Think of the role models, the Dalai Lama, etc., and how they behave.
4. Remember, life is short, so act upon the nine items listed above.

NINE

Believe.

Either death is a state of nothingness and utter unconsciousness, or there is a migration of the soul from this world to another.
— SOCRATES

Happiness comes from spiritual wealth, not material wealth.
— JOHN TEMPLETON

Believing in *something* makes you happier. Why is that? And the next question is: Believe in what?

Why should you need to believe in anything? In short, you don't. But you will lead a happier life if you believe in a system that explains how the world works and your place in it. We'll get into why that is in a minute.

First, let's review the usual suspects. For most people in the world, believing in something means following a religion, Christianity, Judaism, Islam, Hinduism or Buddhism. The first four are based on a single God. Buddhism lacks a creator God and can also be seen as spiritual philosophy—but something that requires belief and study. For Americans, more than 90% believe in God or some sort of higher being.

I will use the words "God" or "religion" in this section, but they refer to any system of belief in a higher order—hopefully one that explains man's purpose, place and meaning in the universe.

Believing and Happiness

But why is a belief in some religion or higher order linked to your happiness?

There's one very obvious reason why happiness and belief are linked: the *afterlife*—or reincarnation in the case of Hinduism and Buddhism. If you don't believe in life after death, things can look pretty grim. At the end of your life, you're put in a box and that's that. Having faith that there is an afterlife is comforting and calming. Someone or something will be there to greet you when the lights go out. You don't need to fear your end. At least, you don't need to fear it as much. Reducing anxiety is a good thing.

Love is another reason religion helps. Most religions, unless unscrupulous people misrepresent them, promote a brotherly love. The act of forgiveness is implicit or explicit throughout mainstream religions. And as we've examined, loving, accepting, respecting and forgiving yourself and others is key part of happiness. Many of the texts teach varying forms of the "Golden Rule": Treat your neighbor as you would like to be treated. This, of course, promotes harmony and reduces conflict. These two points alone are the most powerful arguments to believe, but there are more.

Authentic *freedom*, another key component of happiness, is also linked to religious belief. In Key Two: "Choose Real Freedom," we reviewed how we think we are free but in reality are enslaved by our endless and largely uncontrolled desires. You do not need to find religion to overcome this plight, but it sure helps. As we discussed, Christianity focuses on these superficial wants and aims to replace them with a real truth, a truth that sets you free from earthly desires. And Buddhism's fundamental premise is that man is unhappy because his desires can never be fulfilled. Buddha's goal is to create a freer and, thus, happier life for you.

Belief and Virtue

Another less obvious reason why happiness and belief are linked is order. What does "order" mean? Quite simply it means that if you believe in God or some spiritual system, the world makes sense. The world has a structure and meaning. The universe's was started for a reason. The planets the moon and the stars are part of a larger scheme. The animals and plants were put here on purpose. Humans were given a specific nature and deposited on earth to live their lives according to a higher order. In short, you are here for a reason, part of a larger plan that all fits together. Everything makes sense. Again, this knowledge gives you comfort and an ability to focus on your day-to-day affairs. Instead of worrying about whether anything makes sense, you are freed to spend time working on how you can maximize your happiness.

Does the universe have structure and meaning?

Take this out of the picture and all that changes. Everything is suddenly random and chaotic. How did the universe begin? No one can explain it. And what about the far reaches of the universe. Is it finite? If so, what is beyond the universe? If not, how is infinite space possible? No one has a clue. Even Greek philosophers, who did not have a concept of a single God, attributed the beginning of the universe to some unknown, "prime mover," or God-like force.

If humans, animals and plants just developed out of mud puddles—without some heavenly being guiding their growth—then everything is random. There is no plan. Humans are no different than animals. They may have bigger brains or a specific genetic nature, but that's it. We can't claim to be special, to have a soul that will enter into an afterlife or be reincarnated. And when they close the lid on us, that really is it.

Not believing in a higher order or God has other devastating effects. After all, if we are no different than animals, why should we behave any differently? Philosophers have spent a lot of time on this question, but the bottom line is that not one of them has come up with an answer. Absent God or some higher order, why should you be moral? We lose the foundation of our moral system.

Dostoevsky put it well. He said that when we don't believe, man is free to be evil. G. K. Chesterton similarly said: "When people stop believing in God, they don't believe in nothing—they believe in anything."

Yes, over thousands of years very good arguments have been made about why we should behave even if "someone" isn't watching. But the dirty little secret is that all the arguments that tried to create a moral system without God, a religion or some spiritual order as a basis have failed. Take, for example, the most simple of the arguments, the "Golden Rule": We should treat others as we wish to be treated. Can't we just agree that this is a good thing we should do? Can't we argue that it is our nature to be altruistic? The latest scientific evidence seems to support this view. And can't we assert that if we are virtuous that it will make us happier—as we reviewed in Key Six? The short answer to all these questions is yes. Logic, common sense and experience support these answers. And in the end, you will be happier if you act virtuously.

That said, the truth remains that there is no absolute philosophical proof of the question: Why be moral? You can point out all the obvious arguments above. But the problem is that someone can always disagree. What if an individual doesn't care about harming himself or others? In fact, let's say he wants to stab you for your wallet.

His questions might go something like this: "Why shouldn't I stab you?"

"Because it's wrong," you would respond.

"Why?" he asks.

"Because its against the law," you say.

"But the law is just based on a moral system. And I don't believe in your moral system. You just made it up. You decided that stabbing people was bad. Why?" he says.

"Well. How about because you wouldn't want to be treated that way either?"

"Actually," he says, "I don't care. Stab me. Go ahead . . . Try it. I am stronger, I will win. My moral system is that the strongest and most violent shall rule. Whatever I say is what is what is right and wrong."

And that's just it. Without some basis for right and wrong, without accepted laws and morals, the strong will rule. You could say it is against human nature to behave that way, as the ancient Greeks did—they came the closest to finding a rational basis for morality. But someone could just as easily deny that. They could even deny there is such a thing as a human nature—that we are preprogrammed to seek happiness. They could even say that we all live in a dream and that nothing is real. You might be able to do a decent job of defending it if you had a PhD in meta-ethics. But if you can't defend the moral system, you can't defend the laws, the structure of the society, or the basic human decencies we all take for granted. We would be doomed to live in a world of chaos and anarchy, where the strong ruled.

And if that were true, you could be in immediate physical danger. If someone doesn't believe it's wrong to murder, they could kill you.

But nearly as important as your physical safety is the impact this has on your happiness. Our moral system, as we reviewed in Key Six: "Be

Virtuous," instructs you how to be happy. It informs you that you should love yourself as well as others. It instructs you to pursue the calling that best fits your nature, to live in the present, to learn how to become freer, and to cherish friends and family. If there is no moral system, if everything is relative or just a matter of interpretation, then everything is indeed meaningless. Suddenly, there seems to be less reason why you should follow the virtues we reviewed earlier, which all help you move toward a more contented life.

In that world, we could question the very existence of a state called happiness. We could say it's an illusion that gullible people fall for.

[Note: But even if "believing" is not something you want to do, you can still take the position that you think it is in your nature or interest to behave virtuously. This is a reasonable position that many take. And, as we've shown, you will be happier for it.]

So if believing is something that is of interest to you, what are you to do? Let's first establish that this course is not easy. It is not easy to believe.

Take Mother Theresa as an example. We envision her as someone with unshakable faith. But some of her letters, which were recently released, paint a more complex picture. At 32, she felt called by the voice of God to go into the streets of Calcutta to aid the lepers and the poor. The voice was personal and clear. It was as if she were speaking directly with God and it went on for several years until one day it stopped abruptly. Her letters reveal that she felt an overwhelming sense of abandonment. She struggled to go on. She wrote of the "terrible pain of loss, of God not wanting me, of God not being God, of God not really existing."

She asked her spiritual director how she could go on. The director asked how long it had been since she heard the voice. Mother Theresa said, years. The director responded that it had been many years since she had heard the voice of God. So Mother Theresa returned to the streets again. She wrote how she focused gathering strength and faith by working with the poorest of the poor—seeing God in their faces.

Take Action

And similar to the other keys, the most important point is that belief is *action*. Believing is not just about thinking good thoughts. Whether you are a Buddhist, Jew, Christian or whatever, your beliefs are just a guide to behavior. And behavior reinforces belief. For example, Mother Theresa's helping the poor was just a way of demonstrating and reinforcing her faith. Similarly, Buddhist monks meditate. And when they are and their master senses that a young monk has lost his concentration, he whacks the student on the back with a stick. It may seem odd, but this action helps the monk focus. He becomes stronger in his quest and his belief.

In the end, the French philosopher Pascal put it rather well. He developed Pascal's Wager. He bet that it was better to believe in God, because if you're right you go to heaven and if you're wrong, you'll never know it. The added benefit here is that if you believed, you likely led a happier life as well.

In Review

1. You'll be happier if you believe.
2. Why? Because:
    a. An afterlife is better than no afterlife.
    b. Religions = love and love = happiness.
    c. You can avoid imprisonment by superficial desires.

d. Without belief in an order beyond human kind, moral systems collapse.
3. It's not easy. Even Mother Theresa struggled with massive doubt.
4. Take action: Believing is not just an intellectual process; it is what you do.

TEN

Take Action.

Action may not always bring happiness; but there is no happiness without action.
— Benjamin Disraeli

Happiness is a sort of action.
— Aristotle

Happiness *is* action.

What does that mean? Happiness is not about sitting around and thinking. Happiness is about doing. It is about getting up and going. It is about living. It is about interacting with other people. You are what you do. Your actions define you.

Another way of saying this is that you are your habits. And habits are really nothing more than actions you tend to repeat. What you do over and over defines who you are. Think about that. If you are fat, you overeat. Not once or twice, but thousands of times. If you are kind, you are nice to others. Not sometimes, but almost all the time. It is who you are.

Think about what you do over and over, from week-to-week. Do you get up late? Early? Are you kind to your parents? Do you help your friends? Do you exercise? Do you apply yourself at your job? Are you superficial? Genuine? Vain? Modest? Courageous? A coward? Honest? A liar? Generous? Stingy? Loving? Truthful? Just?

You are your habits.

We like to kid ourselves, when we do something we know we shouldn't. We say, "That's not really me. This is really just an exception. I am going to change, really." But time goes by and we repeat the same behavior. Be honest. That is who you are. Repetitive actions define you.

All the previous keys are just ideas. In fact, this book is just a bunch of ideas. They'll mean nothing to you unless you act upon them. And without doubt that also means changing the way you live your life. And you can do it just that simply — by acting and repeating those actions. Form new habits.

You can sit back and obsess about all the traumas in your life, about what your parents did to you, how your friends treated you, how your girlfriend or boyfriend dumped you, how your career is in a stall, about how overweight you are, how you are anxious around people, how tired you are, and on and on.

The dirty little secret is that you like these traumas and you don't even it know it. They are your friends. They provide you with excuses to do nothing.

God forbid you had no excuses, that you had to act and you failed. Then who would you blame? Excuses are a way of doing nothing. But it's certainly no way to live your life and its certainly no way to get on your way to happiness. Change happens in a moment. You decide to stop eating. You decide to love yourself. You decide to be more confident. You decide to pursue your calling. And on and on.

Let's look at the previous keys and review how each one demands some kind of action. Do these repetitively until they are reflexive. Then you will be a different person and, hopefully, a happier one.

1. *Embrace your limited time.* This key is about waking up. It is about acknowledging that you don't have much time left. You need to realize in the years you have before your death, you must act if you are to be happy. If you only have x amount of time left you better start doing. Doing what? Acting on the rest of these keys. Loving, living, being good/virtuous and pursing your calling.

2. *Choose real freedom.* This key is about choosing well. We are imprisoned by all our desires. We never attain these desires so we remain dissatisfied and unhappy. But we need to recognize these are false desires. They will never make us happy. We attain true freedom by choosing correctly. Choosing is a kind of action. We choose to eat less. We choose not to cheat on our partners. We choose to give up lusting after dollars. We choose not to be satisfied with the material things we have. We choose to limit our desires because that brings freedom and happiness.

3. *Pursue your calling.* This key is about being true to yourself. It is all about action. It is about what you choose to do with your life. You may not have been sure what your calling was at a young age, but you may have a better idea now. If you do, it is up to you to do something about it. Change your career. Start a hobby. Take a risk. Be true to yourself. If your responsibilities keep you from pursuing your true interest, make sure you are being honest. Make sure you really need all the material things your current position brings. If you decide you need to stay put, then use your free time more effectively to pursue your interests. And if you aren't sure what you should do, you still need to take action:

Investigate old interests. Try them. Fail. Try again. Life is about striving — it's about action!

4. *Cherish family and friends.* This key is about reaching out to those closest to you. You've taken them for granted. You may have even used them — a bad action. You need to act better. Take some flowers to your parents. Take them out to dinner. Go see them, if they don't live with you. Take your brother or sister out to lunch. Buy them a present for no reason. Take your spouse on an unannounced trip. Bring them a little gift. Cook dinner yourself. Clean up the house and expect nothing in return, ever. If you need to, choose new friends — those you want to become like. Help an existing friend. Get them a book on their favorite hobby. All these actions will make *you* happier. But your motivation should be the other, not yourself. Do these actions for their own sake.

5. *Live in the present.* This key is about taking control of your life. It is about no longer being a victim. It's about refusing to be imprisoned by your past and paralyzed by your future. It is about enjoying the moment. It is about taking your watch off on the weekends. It's about enjoying your morning shower without your brain running through your daily worries. It's about enjoying the friends and family around you at dinner or on a weekend. It's about taking a walk with your kids. It's about sitting down and staring at a swaying tree. It's about being in the moment. But most of all it's about telling your brain to shut up so you can be in the moment.

6. *Be virtuous.* This key is about being good. You aren't being good sitting by yourself, doing nothing. Being good is about doing good. You need to do courageous things, like change jobs. You should be charitable by donating clothing or tutoring an underprivileged child. You need to be friendly by helping your friends

but not expecting them to return the favor. You should display self-control by not eating too many calories. And you should always be just, standing up for those that are wronged. Keep doing these things and you will develop a new character, a disposition toward doing good. That is in line you're your in-born nature and it is the foundation upon which a more deep-seated happiness is built.

7. *Love yourself.* This key is about love. But love is action. How do you show that you don't love yourself — in the proper sense? You might be overeating. You might be putting yourself down in front of others. You might not be taking opportunities because you think you're worthless. And how do you show that you do love yourself? You believe in yourself. You take risks. You take a job you're not sure you can do. You exercise whether you feel like it or not. You eat right. You live in the moment.

8. *Love others.* This key is also about love. Loving others is also about actions. You don't love others by sitting in a room and telling yourself how much you love them. You love them by doing. You love your spouse by cleaning the kitchen or buying flowers. You love your children by hugging them and spending time with them. You love your parents by taking care of them. You love your friends by helping them with tasks and not expecting them to lift a finger for you. Think about the thousands of actions that can show that you love. The more you do, the more able you are to love.

9. *Believe.* This key is about choosing to believe. You might think that believing is something your brain does, that you need not take some action to believe. But the fact is belief is all about action. It's really no different than love. If you believe, it changes how you behave. You act in accordance with God or Buddha, etc. You will act well toward others. You will work in a soup kitchen.

You will donate money to help the poor. You will care for the sick. You will not gossip. You will do good. You will act.

10. *Take Action.* Well, this key speaks for itself. Go do it.

Once you begin acting on these keys you will slowly be transformed. What will happen is that you will slowly develop new habits, new behaviors. Your old, bad, habits will be replaced. Love will replace cynicism. Real friendship will replace loneliness. Enjoying the moment will replace constant worry.

This will not be easy. It's like a diet or any effort that is difficult. It is painful and you will have some backsliding, falling back into your old habits. The point is to persevere. Realize that much good usually comes out of striving and suffering. This is a life long effort. You are deciding to change the way you live your life. You are deciding to take control. You are deciding to act, to form new habits. You are deciding to be happy.

The alternative, as you know, is to do nothing, to spend your time as you have, glide along year-to-year with no real change, be less happy than you could be, and die. Which do you prefer?

Start by reviewing this list daily. Memorize it. Practice it. Slowly change the way you think. Change the way you behave. Follow these keys and you will, over time, become happy. Be patient. But act.

In Review

1. Act.

Epilogue

Great, you read the keys. Now comes your first real critical choice. Are you going to really change? You've past this same point in your life many times before. You've told yourself, this time it's different. This time I really will _____. You fill in the blank. Maybe it was lose weight. Maybe it was love your parents. Maybe it was change careers. Whatever it was, you didn't do it. Or you gave it a half-hearted effort and failed. And that failure reinforced your belief that you are stuck.

Give up your excuses. Your past is past. What will you do today? Will you focus on these keys? Add some others.

A little hint that will help you is: Don't tell anyone. Don't go around bragging about what you plan to do and how great it will be. That's a sure sign you're not serious. Instead, just go do it. It is your secret. A humble and quiet process of change. That is how real change occurs in your life.

And don't worry. You will fail. Many times. But if you keep coming back and trying over and over again, you have understood. Remember the violin player from our introduction: she would have gotten nowhere if she just sat around wishing she had a concert debut. She had to keep focused on practicing, the years of practicing. Just the same, if you just sit around wishing you were happy, you'll get nowhere. Forget about *trying* to be happy. Just follow the Ten Keys for their own sake and happiness will be a by-product. It will take years.

Happiness is a life long effort. And when you are old and tired you can sit down and think back. You will be able to say to yourself: "I was happy."

www.ingramcontent.com/pod-product-compliance
Lightning Source LLC
Chambersburg PA
CBHW071314040426

42444CB00009B/2012